A Kids Book of Fun Facts and Photos on the Life Cycle of the Butterfly.

By

Amanda Ollier

Copyright 2013 Amanda Ollier

This book, from the Kids Look and Learn series is also available in Kindle format.

Paperback Edition: ISBN 1491299053

Amazon Kindle Version: ASIN B00DPYXAPU

Contents

About This Book - A Note for Grown Ups.

This book has been written with children aged 7 to 11 in mind. There are some words which they will probably find difficult at first and this is intentional. Words which may be hard to pronounce have been broken down into 'sound-a-like' syllables to help with pronunciation and confidence building and you'll find these in brackets next to the word.

Vocabulary considered age appropriate by the UK education system has been included; this will help your child to become familiar with new words without even noticing!

At the end of the book is a fun quiz for the child to test their knowledge and you to gauge their understanding. The answers to all the questions are included in the book itself.

If you enjoy this book, please leave a review at Amazon.

Thank you.

Butterflies and Caterpillars.

If you think that butterflies are just colourful little creatures that you see fluttering about in the countryside during the summer, YOU'RE WRONG!

They can be beautiful and you do only see them when the weather is warm, that's true, but they are not always as cute as you might think!

A beautiful Peacock butterfly

This book is all about butterflies and caterpillars and some interesting and surprising things you might not know about them. They are actually extremely clever, some of them are very athletic and some of them are gross!

We don't know exactly how many different types there are, as we haven't discovered them all yet. We know about 20,000 so far though.

We do know that they have been around for a loooooong time. We can tell from fossils that butterflies have been on earth for about 40 to 50 million years. That's even longer than your grandma!

The biggest butterfly is called a Queen Alexandra's Birdwing. Its wings can be up to 31cm across!

A Queen Alexandra's Birdwing

Some butterflies migrate. That means they go from one country to another. The Monarch butterflies fly all the way from Mexico to Canada that's almost 5000km!

Monarch butterflies which fly right across the USA.

The Life Cycle

Butterflies have short lives. Some only live for about a week but they can live to up to a year – unless a hungry bird or spider catches them first!

A butterfly's life is a process divided into four parts.

1. Egg
2. Larva
3. Pupa
4. Imago

Egg

Each type of butterfly has a favourite plant, called a host plant. This is the one they like to eat, where they live and where they lay their eggs.

Butterfly eggs on a leaf.

The female caterpillar tastes the leaves with her feet, yes, her feet! and then lays the eggs on the underneath of a leaf. She sticks them on with a special glue which is very strong. Some eggs are round like footballs, some are more pointy. You might be able to find some in your garden if you look carefully. Look for leaves which have got holes in and you may find some caterpillars or eggs nearby. If you look closely enough you may be able to see the tiny bugs inside their eggs.

This is a close up of an egg!

The eggs normally only take about 10 days to hatch, but if they are laid at the end of the Summer, they will wait until the following Spring. This is to make sure that there is plenty for the little caterpillars to eat.

Larva

Larva (la-vu) is the name for a baby creature that changes into something different when it becomes an adult, like a beetle or a dragonfly.

A butterfly larva is called a caterpillar

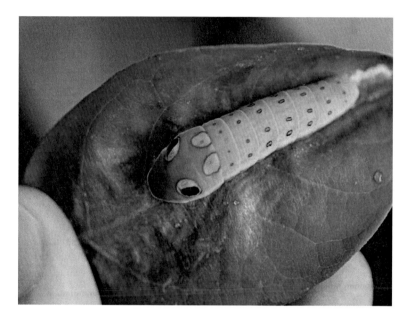

Can you see this caterpillars false eyes?

Can you think of any other creatures that have babies that change into something different when they grow up?

Caterpillars are always hungry and spend most of their life eating. From the moment they are born they eat, which is why the eggs are laid on the plant they like to eat. In fact they eat so much that every now and then they get too big for their skin and it splits and comes off. This is called shedding. Luckily they have new skin underneath!

A hungry caterpillar!

The caterpillars live on the plants that their eggs hatched on, munching away all day. Some of them like things like cabbage and lettuce and can be quite destructive which is why some gardeners don't like caterpillars.

Most caterpillars only eat plants, but some types, like the Harvester butterfly eat other insects, like greenfly too!

Some caterpillars prefer to live with friends. The San Bruno Elfin butterfly lives with ants. The ants protect the caterpillar from other insects and the caterpillar gives the ants a special drink called honeydew, that the ants really love. It's a good swap!

The San Remo Elfin caterpillar lives with ants.

They have long bodies with three pairs of legs at the front. These are called true legs. At the back they have six more pairs of legs. These are called prolegs and they are not actually real legs at all! They are used for gripping instead of walking.

How many pairs of shoes would a caterpillar need?

Caterpillars can be very colourful, just like butterflies and some use their colours and patterns to scare away anyone who might want to eat them. Some, like the Monarch butterfly larva, look like they have a head at both ends to confuse predators.

This is a Monarch caterpillar. Can you tell which end is the head?

Some caterpillars have developed other ways to seem less tasty, to disguise themselves or scare off attackers. Here are a few:

If they think they are about to get eaten, they might sit really still so that they look like a twig or even a bird poo!

Some can make their heads blow up so that they look like a snake.

Some have little horns that they can make pop up on their heads that smell really bad! Yuck! Who wants to eat smelly food?

Smelly horns sticking out. Yuck!

Some have poisonous hairs on their backs, or spots that look like eyes to scare off birds. If you touch a hairy caterpillar you might get a rash on your hands from the hairs.

A very hairy caterpillar!

Pupa

When the caterpillar is quite fat enough, it goes under a leaf and sheds its skin one last time. The new skin has the start of tiny wings underneath it. It goes dry and hard to form a kind of cocoon called a pupa or chrysalis (cris-u-liss).

A chrysalis or cocoon on a leaf

The chrysalis sticks under a leaf, or on a twig to blend in with the environment (en-vir-o-ment) for protection. This disguise helps it to hide from predators who might like to eat the fat tasty caterpillar!

Do you know what a predator is?

A row of chrysalis on a twig.

While the caterpillar is inside the cocoon, it starts to change into a butterfly. This is called metamorphosis (met-u-more-fu-sis). That's just a big word that means changing from one thing into something else, your teacher will like that word!

To protect themselves while they are in the cocoon, pupating, some have learnt to wriggle and some can even make a noise to sound scary!

Can you think of anything that might enjoy this little snack? A ready wrapped caterpillar take away!

The pupa grows tiny folded up wings and its big fat body gets much smaller.

When it is ready, usually after about two weeks, the new butterfly will break out of the chrysalis and stretch its wings out to dry. This can take several hours.

Monarch Butterflies hatching from their cocoon.

You must never help a butterfly to escape from its cocoon. Even though you might think it is kind, this exercise is essential to help pump its wings up and fill them with butterfly blood, which is called hemolymph (he-mo-lim-f) If it doesn't do that it will never be able to fly.

Just like when you have to do things that seem hard so that you can learn to do them by yourself.

See if the grownups you know know what butterfly blood is called.

If it's too near the end of summer, the caterpillar will stay in its cosy cocoon all winter and wait for the warmer weather, just like the eggs.

Imago

An imago (im-aa-go) is the adult creature at the end of metamorphosis. Adult butterflies have four wings and 6 legs. They have two big boggly eyes that can see light that ours can't and two long antennae (an-ten-u) on their head, that they use to sense where their favourite plants are. A bit like we use our nose to smell.

Can you see the 4 wings and antennae?

They use a long hollow tube, like a tongue, called a proboscis (pro-boss-kiss) to feed but they have no mouth. They breathe through holes in their body.

A delicious meal using the proboscis.

Do you remember what the female caterpillar used to taste the leaves with?

The adult butterfly's main job is to lay more eggs for the future generation of caterpillars to grow. As well as this they help us by taking pollen between flowers, like bees do. This happens because butterflies mostly eat nectar, which is a sweet liquid inside flowers. When they poke their long proboscis into the flower to suck out the nectar the pollen sticks to them and then they carry it to the next plant.

Flowers on trees and plants need pollen from other flowers to be able to grow fruit and seeds. This is called pollination and is very important. If there were no bees and butterflies to pollinate our plants, we would run out of some types of food very quickly and no new trees would grow. We need trees to make oxygen for us to breathe and to clean our air, so this is a really important job.

Some butterflies don't only eat nectar though. Some like to eat pollen or tree sap too. Others like to eat rotten fruit and some really gross ones like to eat dead flesh, or to lick the sweat from a hot human and some even eat poo! Yuck!

Their wings are covered in tiny scales which give them the beautiful colours and patterns. If you touch a butterfly you will damage the scales and they won't be able to fly properly anymore, so you should never touch their wings.

A close up picture of a butterfly wing.

Each type of butterfly has a special colour and pattern on their wings. It helps you to tell what type they are. Some of them are very bright and this is part of their protection. Nature warns animals of danger by making things bright colours like red and orange, so some butterflies use these colours so that other things won't eat them!

A Comma butterfly

Others eat the poison from plants and store it up inside them so that they taste nasty! I think I'd prefer the bright colours, wouldn't you?

Like caterpillars, some have spots on their wings that look like eyes. Scientists think that this is so that predators will attack the wrong end and that will give them time to escape!

A Meadow Brown butterfly

One type of butterfly has see-through wings, which makes them harder to spot.

A Glass Wing butterfly

Who would have thought that these little things would be so clever?

You don't see as many butterflies today as you used to, because of pollution, and changes in farming like using chemicals to kill insects and help crops to grow better and removing hedges where the butterflies like to live.

Do you think that's a good idea?

Quiz Time!

If you have enjoyed learning about butterflies and caterpillars, test your new knowledge with this little quiz and see how much you can remember? You may be surprised to see how successful you are!

Question1

How many stages are there in a butterfly's life?

Question 2

Can you name each of the stages in the butterfly's life cycle?

Question 3

Where does the female lay her eggs?

Question 4

What shape are the eggs?

Question 5

How many legs does a caterpillar have?

Question 6

How long have butterflies been on earth?

Question 7

How long do butterflies live?

Question 8

Name some things that butterflies like to eat

Question 9

What is hemolymph?

Question 10

How do caterpillars try to stop themselves being eaten?

Question 11

What does metamorphosis mean?

Question 12

What part of their bodies do butterflies use to taste?

Question 13

What is the thing called that the caterpillar goes into to turn into a butterfly? Clue, it looks a bit like a sleeping bag!

Question 14

What happens when the caterpillar gets too fat?

Question 15

What good things do butterflies do for us?

Question 16

Why mustn't you help them to get out of their chrysalis?

Question 17

How many types of butterfly are there?

Question 18

Can butterflies fly a long way?

Question19

What is a larva?

Question 20

Can you draw a picture of a butterfly? Can you remember some of the things that they have on their wings?

Remember to look out for them when it is warm outside.

If you have enjoyed this book, please leave a great review on Amazon.

About the Author

Amanda Ollier is a Master Practitioner of Neuro Linguistic Programming, Time Line Therapy™ and Hypnosis, who works with children for whom spelling and reading are a challenge.

Using a combination of motivation and proven learning strategies, she is able to help them improve both their test scores and their overall learning experience.

Amanda is also the author of the best selling personal development series The Self Help Bible and co-author of The Mindset Shift.

You can find out more at http://amzn.to/S5TR3N

http://facebook.com/theselfhelpbible

Please leave a review of the book on Amazon. Just type Amanda Ollier into Amazon to find the book!

Thank you!

Made in United States
North Haven, CT
22 April 2022

18467469R00020